# Vocabulary Development for ESL Students

## —— Intermediate Level ——

Lisa Solski

**BRIEF OVERVIEW:** This workbook teaches Intermediate Level ESL students 150 common words to improve conversation, comprehension and writing. Simple strategies incorporate new vocabulary into everyday life situations.

Copyright © On The Mark Press 2018

This publication may be reproduced under licence from Access Copyright, or with the express written permission of On The Mark Press, or as permitted by law. All rights are otherwise reserved, and no part of this publication may be reproduced, stored in a retrieval system, or transmitted in any form or by any means, electronic, mechanical, photocopying, scanning, recording or otherwise, except as specifically authorized.

All Rights Reserved.

Printed in Canada.

Published in Canada by:
On The Mark Press
Belleville, ON
www.onthemarkpress.com

# At A Glance

| Learning Expectations | Recognizes New Words | Uses a dictionary, thesaurus, and personal dictionary. | Uses flash cards and finds a helper to practise pronunciation. | Divides words into syllables. | Examines root words, prefixes, and suffixes. | Uses context when reading. |
|---|---|---|---|---|---|---|
| Recognizes new vocabulary words when they are presented. | ● | | | | | |
| Uses a dictionary, thesaurus and personal dictionary to learn new words. | | ● | | | | |
| Uses flash cards and finds a helper to practise pronunciation. | | | ● | | | |
| Divides words into syllables. | | | | ● | | |
| Examines root words, prefixes, and suffixes. | | | | | ● | |
| Uses context when reading. | | | | | | ● |

# Table of Contents

At a Glance . . . . . . . . . . . . . . . . . . . . . . . . . . . . . . . . . . . . . . . . . . . . . . . . . . 2

Teacher Assessment Rubric . . . . . . . . . . . . . . . . . . . . . . . . . . . . . . . . . . . . 4

Student Self-Assessment Rubric . . . . . . . . . . . . . . . . . . . . . . . . . . . . . . . 5

Acquiring New Vocabulary . . . . . . . . . . . . . . . . . . . . . . . . . . . . . . . . . . . . 6

Follow These ESL Vocabulary Strategies for Each Lesson . . . . . . . . . . . 10

**LESSON 1: SIGNS VOCABULARY** . . . . . . . . . . . . . . . . . . . . . . . . . . . . . . 11

**LESSON 2: TIME ZONES VOCABULARY** . . . . . . . . . . . . . . . . . . . . . . . . 16

**LESSON 3: AUTOMOBILE VOCABULARY** . . . . . . . . . . . . . . . . . . . . . . . 21

**LESSON 4: DRUG STORE VOCABULARY** . . . . . . . . . . . . . . . . . . . . . . . 26

**LESSON 5: INTERNET VOCABULARY** . . . . . . . . . . . . . . . . . . . . . . . . . . 31

**LESSON 6: HOUSING VOCABULARY** . . . . . . . . . . . . . . . . . . . . . . . . . . 36

**LESSON 7: LAUNDRY AND DRY-CLEANING VOCABULARY** . . . . . . . . 41

**LESSON 8: EDUCATION AND CAREER VOCABULARY** . . . . . . . . . . . . 46

**LESSON 9: LAW VOCABULARY** . . . . . . . . . . . . . . . . . . . . . . . . . . . . . . 51

**LESSON 10: GOVERNMENT VOCABULARY** . . . . . . . . . . . . . . . . . . . . . 56

**LESSON 11: JOB AND INTERVIEW VOCABULARY** . . . . . . . . . . . . . . . . 61

**LESSON 12: SOCIAL NETWORKING VOCABULARY** . . . . . . . . . . . . . . 66

**LESSON 13: FITNESS AND HEALTH VOCABULARY** . . . . . . . . . . . . . . 71

**LESSON 14: HOBBIES AND ENTERTAINMENT VOCABULARY** . . . . . . . 76

**LESSON 15: FOOD SAFETY VOCABULARY** . . . . . . . . . . . . . . . . . . . . . 81

Answer Key . . . . . . . . . . . . . . . . . . . . . . . . . . . . . . . . . . . . . . . . . . . . . . 86

# Teacher Assessment Rubric

Student's Name: _____

Put a check mark ✓ in the box that indicates the student's level of achievement.

| Level 1 | requires assistance, inconsistent effort, shows limited understanding of concepts |
|---|---|
| Level 2 | requires minimal assistance, shows limited understanding of concepts |
| Level 3 | independent, consistent effort, shows general understanding of concepts |
| Level 4 | independent, consistent effort, shows thorough understanding of concepts |

| Criteria | Level 1 | Level 2 | Level 3 | Level 4 |
|---|---|---|---|---|
| Recognizes new vocabulary words when they are presented. | | | | |
| Uses a dictionary, thesaurus and Personal Dictionary to learn new words. | | | | |
| Uses flash cards and finds a helper to practise pronunciation. | | | | |
| Divides words into syllables. | | | | |
| Examines root words, prefixes, and suffixes. | | | | |
| Uses context when reading. | | | | |

# Student Self-Assessment Rubric

Name: _____ Date: _____

Put a check mark ✓ in the box that best describes your performance. Then add your points.

| Expectations | 1 Needs Improvement | 2 Sometimes | 3 Frequently | 4 Always/ Usually | Points |
|---|---|---|---|---|---|
| Recognizes new vocabulary words when they are presented. | | | | | |
| Uses a dictionary, thesaurus and Personal Dictionary to learn new words. | | | | | |
| Uses flash cards and finds a helper to practise pronunciation. | | | | | |
| Divides words into syllables. | | | | | |
| Examines root words, prefixes, and suffixes. | | | | | |
| Uses context when reading. | | | | | |

# Acquiring New Vocabulary

Unfamiliar vocabulary prevents English language learners from understanding what they read. Chances are they often ask themselves questions like this when they read.

- What is this word?
- Have I ever seen this word before?
- What are the parts of this word?
- What does this word mean?
- How should I use this word when writing?

This book is designed to help English learners become more successful in understanding and using English words. Experts agree that **reading, writing, speaking and listening** are the keys to developing a better vocabulary. One of the many frustrations students encounter when **reading** new material is unfamiliar vocabulary. It is not uncommon while **reading** a passage for students to come across several unfamiliar words that prevent them from understanding the passage, not to mention the frustration it causes. Then, when **writing**, they have to create ideas and organize them into meaningful phrases, clauses and sentences that others can understand. **Writing** also requires proper punctuation, grammar and spelling. In order to use these essential skills, an acceptable level of vocabulary is needed. When **listening**, students have to pay attention to the words and try to interpret the meanings. Often, this involves several processes happening at once. Finally, when **speaking**, students have to think ahead about how to respond appropriately in conversations. This chart asks students to answer yes or no to these questions.

## Rate Yourself

Rate yourself on how you feel about your own English vocabulary. Answer yes or no.

| Yes | No | |
|---|---|---|
| | | Frequently, I encounter words that I cannot pronounce or do not understand. |
| | | Repeating new words and using a dictionary or thesaurus helps improve my vocabulary. |
| | | When my teacher uses pictures, flash cards and other activities, I feel like I am learning new words more easily. |
| | | Using a dictionary helps me understand new words. It also helps me see how words are pronounced and broken down into syllables. |
| | | Reading introduces me to new words and helps improve my vocabulary. |

Acquiring New Vocabulary

## Find Mentors or Other Helpers!

It is very important to practise new skills every day, and it does not have to happen alone. Finding a learning partner or mentor is an ideal way to practise vocabulary and build confidence. Also, when learners are given opportunities in class to interact with each other in this way, learning happens even more easily. If needed, tutors can help as well. There are several other ways to build vocabulary such as volunteering for organizations and businesses at jobs that require conversation. These methods quickly provide rewards in learning and take place in a natural setting. They provide the learner with valuable opportunities to use the English language to improve speaking, and enhance vocabulary. Public libraries frequently offer conversation classes, as well, in which people can simply get together with others to practise English.

## Practising Clear Speech

There are many ways to practise pronunciation, and it is important to recognize that clear speech is extremely important. At home, reading aloud and recording articles from text or online sources and reviewing the recordings to make changes helps learners speak more effectively. Online websites are great places to learn more effective speech through listening and practising important sounds and phrases. It is a great way to learn alone or in groups. Some websites are very advanced and allow students to listen, read, record, receive feedback and practise in unique ways.

## Reading For Thirty Minutes Daily Is Essential

One of the most effective ways to learn new vocabulary is by reading regularly, and frequently. Busy students benefit by setting aside thirty minutes at the end of the day for reading. The internet is the preferred method of reading today, and there are several websites with reading material geared to teaching new vocabulary. These websites contain a variety of formats including novels, short stories, poems, news articles, etc. Moreover, tackling new information while learning is also beneficial. Summarizing and paraphrasing the main ideas and key points while reading helps tremendously. By setting aside a short period of time each day to read, learners will soon begin to reap the benefits.

## Syllabication

The vowels are **a, e, i, o** and **u**. Sometimes, **y** and **w** are also considered vowel sounds. Syllables are the sounds heard when these words are pronounced, and they contain separate sounds. The number of syllables in a word is the number of times the listener hears a vowel sound. For example, in the word **dog**, there is one syllable—the sound of

> Acquiring New Vocabulary

the short vowel **o**. In the word **puppy**, there are two syllables—the sound of the short vowel **u** and the sound of the vowel sound **y** (pronounced **long- e**). Dictionaries separate words into syllables using hyphens or dots. Dividing new words into syllables while reading is a helpful exercise not to be overlooked. It is amazing how quickly new words can become part of everyday vocabulary by practising this activity.

**To Divide Words into Syllables:**

- Divide words after prefixes: un-clean;
- Divide words before suffixes: express-ing;
- Divide words between double consonants: fos-sil;
- For words with long vowel sounds, divide after the vowel: slo-gan;
- For words with short vowel sounds: divide after the consonant: sev-en.

## Prefixes/ Suffixes/Root Words

### Prefixes

Prefixes are letters or groups of letters added to the beginnings of words; they change the meanings of the words. Common prefixes are **re, ex,** and **pre**. For example, learners probably use the word **redo** frequently. What does **redo** mean? By breaking the word into syllables, it can be seen that **do** means to perform an activity. By adding the prefix **re**, which means **to do again**, the meaning changes. It is evident that knowing the meaning of a prefix and the root word, can help in figuring out the meanings of many new words. Other widely used prefixes include **un, in** and **dis**.

### Suffixes

Suffixes are letters or groups of letters that appear at the endings of words. Like prefixes, suffixes change the meanings of words. Furthermore, as a suffix is added to a word, the word changes from one format or part of speech to another. For example, the suffix **ment** means a state of being or particular place. By adding **ment** to the verb **establish**, the word **establishment** results, which means a location where people carry out different procedures. Common suffixes include **ment, tion, ly**. By taking time to break words down into words and suffixes, they are easier to learn, use and remember.

### Root Words

Root words are the main or basic parts of words, and these basic parts contain the meanings of the words. For example, the root word **care** means having or showing concern. Other words develop from this basic word such as **careful**, **careless** and

> Acquiring New Vocabulary

**carefully**. Sometimes, words contain more than one root word such as **popcorn (pop and corn)** and **fireman (fire and man)**. Since root words contain the meaning of words, it is important to use these roots to help unlock the meaning of other words. Students will be amazed at the number of words they can add to their vocabularies by studying root words and their meanings. Grammar books and online sources often contain lists of root words and their meanings that help learners acquire this skill. It quickly helps with the identification of the meanings of many words and recognizes the relationships with other languages, as well.

## Learning Words From Context

Using context means using words and sentences situated **close to the sentence in question** to decipher the meaning of a word or expression. By examining the nearby words and sentences, it is possible to figure out the meaning of new words as well as entire sentences. A good strategy is to read through the entire sentence and search for the key words as they are good clues to meaning. Another strategy is to read the sentences before and after the sentence or phrase in question as they also contain meaningful clues. These clues are called context clues. It is good practise to read back at least two sentences and forward at least one sentence while searching for clues.

Now let's practise. Look through this sentence to find the key words as they contain valuable clues to the meaning. Read this sentence. **After paying off all of their credit cards, the young couple felt like a tremendous load had been taken off their shoulders.** By determining the meaning of the word, **tremendous** (massive, huge, monumental), it is possible to see that the sentence means that the young couple feel that the pressure of the credit cards no longer exists.

## Summary:

- Repetition is important, so practise words in different ways.
- Carry and use a dictionary and thesaurus (print or online).
- Make and use flash cards and a personal dictionary.
- Regularly practise clear speech.
- Read on a daily basis.
- Study format: Divide words into syllables, locate root words, prefixes and suffixes of words.

# Follow these steps for each lesson.

1. **REPETITION:** Repeat the word aloud several times.

2. **READ:** Read the vocabulary words and definitions.

3. **MATCH:** Match the new word or sentence to the picture.

4. **PERSONAL DICTIONARY:** Create your own personal dictionary. On each page, include:
   a. A dictionary definition
   b. A sample sentence
   c. An original sentence

5. **READ:** Read daily for at least 30 minutes.

6. **PRACTISE:** Examine prefixes, suffixes, and root words and find new words that contain the same patterns.

9. **CONTEXT:** Use context clues to help you learn new words.

10. **DICTIONARY and THESAURUS:** Keep these tools handy, and use them frequently.

# Lesson 1: Signs Vocabulary

Look at the illustration. What do you think the vocabulary words mean? Predict a meaning based on the illustration.

| # | Vocabulary Words | Predicted Meaning | Illustration |
|---|---|---|---|
| 1. | men at work | _____ _____ _____ | |
| 2. | school crossing | _____ _____ _____ | |
| 3. | high water level | _____ _____ _____ | |
| 4. | handicapped parking | _____ _____ _____ | |
| 5. | dogs on leash | _____ _____ _____ | |

**Lesson 1**  Signs Vocabulary  Name:

| # | Vocabulary Words | Predicted Meaning | Illustration |
|---|---|---|---|
| 6. | thin ice | _____ _____ _____ | Danger Thin Ice |
| 7. | do not pass | _____ _____ _____ | |
| 8. | hill warning | _____ _____ _____ | |
| 9. | detour | _____ _____ _____ | DETOUR → |
| 10. | watch for wildlife | _____ _____ _____ | WILDLIFE XING |

**Lesson 1** — Signs Vocabulary        Name:

## Fill in the Blanks:

Use the vocabulary words to fill in the blanks with the correct answers. Use each answer once.

| speed bumps | school crossing | high water level | handicapped parking | dogs on leash |
| merge | Do not pass. | steep hill warning | detour | Watch for wildlife. |

1. Since it rained, there is a _____ warning beside the pond today.

2. To avoid receiving a fine from the city, it is better to obey the _____ sign in the neighbourhood.

3. Since the _____ went into effect, there are fewer cars breaking the speed limit.

4. _____ on this road as there is a lot of oncoming traffic.

5. We will have to take a _____ because the main road is closed due to forest fires.

6. Be careful at the _____, especially before and after school.

7. Mother said she noticed a deer lately, so let's _____.

8. It is a long distance to the front door, so be sure to use the _____.

9. I don't like having to _____ during peak hours because some drivers are so discourteous.

10. Right before the steep upgrade, there is a _____.

**Lesson 1**   Signs Vocabulary                                   Name:

## Find the Meaning:

Match the Vocabulary Words with the meanings. Write the correct letter in the answer column.

| # | Vocabulary Words | Answer | Meanings |
|---|---|---|---|
| 1. | speed bumps | | a. The water level is high and dangerous. |
| 2. | school crossing | | b. Dogs must be kept on leashes in public places. |
| 3. | high water level | | c. Vehicles must not pass each other. |
| 4. | handicapped parking | | d. The regular route is closed. |
| 5. | dogs on leash | | e. bumps in the road to prevent speeding |
| 6. | thin ice | | f. space reserved for handicapped individuals |
| 7. | Do not pass. | | g. Children are crossing the street. |

**Lesson 1**  Signs Vocabulary  Name:

| # | Vocabulary Words | Answer | Meanings |
|---|---|---|---|
| 8. | steep hill warning | _____ | h. The ice is thin and dangerous. |
| 9. | detour | _____ | i. There is a hill ahead with a steep angle. |
| 10. | Watch for wildlife. | _____ | j. wildlife nearby and they may cross streets |

*Congratulations! You have completed this lesson.*

Circle the words containing prefixes or suffixes.

1. wildlife    level          thin        dangerous
2. detour      handicapped    steep       crossing
3. leashes     public         vehicles    parking

**Lesson 2**

# Lesson 2: Time Zones Vocabulary

Look at the illustration. What do you think the vocabulary words mean? Predict a meaning based on the illustration.

| # | Vocabulary Words | Predicted Meaning | Illustration |
|---|---|---|---|
| 1. | Pacific Time | _____ _____ _____ | |
| 2. | Mountain Time | _____ _____ _____ | |
| 3. | Central Time | _____ _____ _____ | |
| 4. | Eastern Time | _____ _____ _____ | |
| 5. | Atlantic Time | _____ _____ _____ | |

Source: timeanddate.com

**Lesson 2**  Time Zones Vocabulary                    Name:

| # | Vocabulary Words | Predicted Meaning | Illustration |
|---|---|---|---|
| 6. | Newfoundland Time | | |
| 7. | Standard Time | | |
| 8. | Daylight Time | | |
| 9. | Time Zone | | |
| 10. | Yukon Time | | |

Source: timeanddate.com

**Lesson 2** Time Zones Vocabulary   Name:

## Fill in the Blanks:

Use the vocabulary words to fill in the blanks with the correct answers. Use each answer once.

| Pacific Time | Mountain Time | Central Time | Eastern Time | Atlantic Time |
| Newfoundland Time | Standard Time | time zones | Yukon Time | Daylight Time |

1. Most people like _____ because it doesn't get dark until late in the evening.

2. When we lived in Montreal, we followed _____.

3. My daughter learned the definition of _____ today in Social Studies class.

4. Set your watches and clocks to _____ when you move to Calgary.

5. _____ is the only time zone that is one-half hour later than other zones.

6. My relatives who live in the Yukon, follow _____.

7. The television said the time was given in _____.

8. My grandmother who called from Winnipeg said they use _____.

9. _____ hasn't been used for years now.

10. In Halifax, isn't time read in _____?

**Lesson 2**  Time Zones Vocabulary          Name:

## Find the Meaning:

Match the Vocabulary Words with the meanings. Write the correct letter in the answer column.

| # | Vocabulary Words | Answer | Meanings |
|---|---|---|---|
| 1. | Pacific Time | ___ | a. time zone used in Nova Scotia, New Brunswick, Prince Edward Island and parts of Quebec and Labrador |
| 2. | Mountain Time | ___ | b. time zone used in most of Quebec and parts of Ontario and Nunavut |
| 3. | Central Time | ___ | c. time zone used in parts of Ontario, Manitoba, Saskatchewan and Nunavut |
| 4. | Eastern Time | ___ | d. time zone used in Newfoundland and parts of Labrador |
| 5. | Atlantic Time | ___ | e. the local time in a particular area or region |
| 6. | Newfoundland Time | ___ | f. time zone used in Alberta, parts of Saskatchewan, British Columbia, and the Northwest Territories |
| 7. | Standard Time | ___ | g. time zone used in Yukon, most of British Columbia and parts of the Northwest Territories |

**Lesson 2** Time Zones Vocabulary   Name:

| # | Vocabulary Words | Answer | Meanings |
|---|---|---|---|
| 8. | Daylight Time | _____ | h. an area or region that follows a particular time |
| 9. | time zone | _____ | i. putting the clock ahead one hour in the summer to make the days appear longer |
| 10. | Yukon Time | _____ | j. time zone that has been changed; residents now follow Pacific *Time* |

**Congratulations! You have completed this lesson.**

Circle the correct answer.

1. The province of Alberta follows the _____ time zone.
    a. Central
    b. Pacific
    c. Mountain

2. The city of Montreal follows the _____ time zone.
    a. Atlantic
    b. Central
    c. Eastern

Source: timeanddate.com

# Lesson 3: Automobile Vocabulary

Look at the illustration. What do you think the vocabulary words mean? Predict a meaning based on the illustration.

| # | Vocabulary Words | Predicted Meaning | Illustration |
|---|---|---|---|
| 1. | oil check | | |
| 2. | vehicle registration | | |
| 3. | snow tires | | |
| 4. | model | | |
| 5. | liability insurance | | |

| Lesson 3 | Automobile Vocabulary | | Name: |

| # | Vocabulary Words | Predicted Meaning | Illustration |
|---|---|---|---|
| 6. | collision insurance | | |
| 7. | defroster | | |
| 8. | sedan | | |
| 9. | jumper cables | | |
| 10. | sport utility vehicle (SUV) | | |

**Lesson 3** Automobile Vocabulary    Name:

## Fill in the Blanks:

Use the vocabulary words to fill in the blanks with the correct answers. Use each answer once.

| oil check | vehicle registration | snow tires | model | liability insurance |
|---|---|---|---|---|
| collision insurance | defroster | sedan | jumper cables | sport utility vehicle (SUV) |

1. My dad always carries _____ in his trunk in case his battery goes dead.

2. Please turn on the _____ if the windows become foggy.

3. I know this car is a Toyota, but which _____?

4. I forgot to fill out my _____ this year, so the government sent me a notice.

5. You had a two-door car before, why did you change to a _____?

6. There is a snowfall warning, so let's put on our _____.

7. I think a Rav4 is classified as an _____.

8. Taxi drivers need good _____.

9. When I rolled the truck, I was pleased that I had purchased _____.

10. When you go to the garage, ask the mechanic to do an _____.

**Lesson 3** Automobile Vocabulary  Name:

## Find the Meaning:

Match the Vocabulary Words with the meanings. Write the correct letter in the answer column.

| # | Vocabulary Words | Answer | Meanings |
|---|---|---|---|
| 1. | oil check | | a. a vehicle that contains the inner workings of a truck but is used as a car |
| 2. | vehicle registration | | b. checking to see if the car needs oil |
| 3. | snow tires | | c. paying a fee on a yearly basis to register the vehicle with the government |
| 4. | model | | d. cables that an owner can attach to the battery of another vehicle in order to start a vehicle |
| 5. | liability insurance | | e. a type of insurance that protects the owner when the vehicle is damaged |
| 6. | collision insurance | | f. This piece of equipment keeps the windshield clear. |
| 7. | defroster | | g. special tires used to make winter driving safer |

**Lesson 3** Automobile Vocabulary  Name:

| # | Vocabulary Words | Answer | Meanings |
|---|---|---|---|
| 8. | sedan | _____ | h. one design in a line of cars |
| 9. | jumper cables | _____ | i. a type of insurance that protects the owners from lawsuits |
| 10. | sport utility vehicle (SUV) | _____ | j. a car with four doors |

*Congratulations! You have completed this lesson.*

Answer these questions in complete sentences.

1. What is the difference between collision and liability insurance?

   _____

   _____

   _____

2. What is the difference between a sedan and a sport utility vehicle (SUV)?

   _____

   _____

   _____

# Lesson 4: Drug Store Vocabulary

Look at the illustration. What do you think the vocabulary words mean? Predict a meaning based on the illustration.

| # | Vocabulary Words | Predicted Meaning | Illustration |
|---|---|---|---|
| 1. | Store the medication at room temperature. | | |
| 2. | may cause drowsiness | | |
| 3. | Avoid direct sunlight. | | |
| 4. | expires January, 2018 | | |
| 5. | refills 0 | | |

**Lesson 4** — Drug Store Vocabulary         Name:

| # | Vocabulary Words | Predicted Meaning | Illustration |
|---|---|---|---|
| 6. | one capsule three times a day | _____ _____ _____ | |
| 7. | generic | _____ _____ _____ | |
| 8. | dropper | _____ _____ _____ | |
| 9. | over the counter | _____ _____ _____ | |
| 10. | syringe | _____ _____ _____ | |

**Lesson 4** Drug Store Vocabulary    Name:

## Fill in the Blanks:

Use the vocabulary words to fill in the blanks with the correct answers. Use each answer once.

| Store the medication at room temperature. | may cause drowsiness | Avoid direct sunlight. | expires January, 2018 | refills 0 |
| one capsule three times a day | generic name | dropper | over the counter | syringe |

1. The label on the liquid anti-biotic says to _____.

2. Go to the doctor for a new prescription because the bottle says _____.

3. The doctor injected the medicine into my arm using a _____.

4. Take _____.

5. Make sure the _____ is clean before you put it near your eyes.

6. We might have to stay inside to _____.

7. That prescription _____, so we will need a new one then.

8. My sister didn't want to drive to work because the doctor told her the cough medicine _____.

9. That medicine can be purchased by prescription or _____.

10. Is that the _____ or the trade name for that capsule?

**Lesson 4** — Drug Store Vocabulary   Name:

## Find the Meaning:

Match the Vocabulary Words with the meanings. Write the correct letter in the answer column.

| # | Vocabulary Words | Answer | Meanings |
|---|---|---|---|
| 1. | Store the medication at room temperature. | | a. Keep the medication at a comfortable temperature. |
| 2. | may cause drowsiness | | b. The drug store will not give you another prescription. |
| 3. | Avoid direct sunlight. | | c. a tiny tube and plunger that work together to insert liquid into parts of the body |
| 4. | expires January, 2018 | | d. drugs that can be purchased without a prescription |
| 5. | no refills | | e. may make you feel sleepy |
| 6. | one capsule three times a day | | f. Do not become exposed to the sun. |
| 7. | generic | | g. drugs without a brand name |

**Lesson 4** Drug Store Vocabulary  Name:

| # | Vocabulary Words | Answer | Meanings |
|---|---|---|---|
| 8. | dropper | _____ | h. a small piece of equipment used for placing small drops of liquid into parts of the body such as the nose or eyes |
| 9. | over the counter | _____ | i. Do not take this medicine after this date. |
| 10. | syringe | _____ | j. Take this capsule at three different times during the day. |

*Congratulations! You have completed this lesson.*

Circle the words that are spelled incorrectly.

sryinge        generic        droper        counter

medciation     drowsyness     capsule       direct

# Lesson 5: Internet Vocabulary

Look at the illustration. What do you think the vocabulary words mean? Predict a meaning based on the illustration.

| # | Vocabulary Words | Predicted Meaning | Illustration |
|---|---|---|---|
| 1. | Internet | | |
| 2. | World Wide Web | | |
| 3. | server | | |
| 4. | router | | |
| 5. | modem | | |

| Lesson 6 | Internet Vocabulary | | Name: |
|---|---|---|---|

| # | Vocabulary Words | Predicted Meaning | Illustration |
|---|---|---|---|
| 6. | Web browser | _____ _____ _____ | |
| 7. | search engine | _____ _____ _____ | |
| 8. | network | _____ _____ _____ | |
| 9. | Internet Service Provider (ISP) | _____ _____ _____ | |
| 10. | HTTP/HTML | _____ _____ _____ | |

**Lesson 5** — Internet Vocabulary     Name:

## Fill in the Blanks:

Use the vocabulary words to fill in the blanks with the correct answers. Use each answer once.

| Internet | World Wide Web (WWW) | server | router | modem |
| --- | --- | --- | --- | --- |
| Web browser | search engine | network | Internet Service Provider (ISP) | HTTP/HTML |

1. Every morning, I sign into that _____ when I go to the gym.

2. The notice says that the _____ will be down for awhile.

3. Did you connect the _____ to the modem?

4. We changed our _____ in order to get a better rate on internet service.

5. Use this _____ to find the websites you need for your project.

6. We will be using the _____ to help us in our research projects.

7. Sending emails is one of my favourite aspects of using the _____.

8. My sister learned about _____ in the course she is taking at college.

9. We are going to purchase a faster _____ to increase the speed of our computer.

10. Do you use Microsoft Internet Explorer as your _____?

**Lesson 5** | Internet Vocabulary | Name:

## Find the Meaning:

Match the Vocabulary Words with the meanings. Write the correct letter in the answer column.

| # | Vocabulary Words | Answer | Meanings |
|---|---|---|---|
| 1. | Internet | | a. a network used worldwide that connects computers and information |
| 2. | World Wide Web (WWW) | | b. a wired or wireless device that connects computers |
| 3. | server | | c. the part of the Internet that displays web pages |
| 4. | router | | d. a company that provides internet services for a fee |
| 5. | modem | | e. short for hypertext transfer protocol and hypertext markup language |
| 6. | web browser | | f. several computers working together to share data and information |
| 7. | search engine | | g. a network of information and content that people can gain access to over the Internet |

**Lesson 5**  Internet Vocabulary    Name:

| # | Vocabulary Words | Answer | Meanings |
|---|---|---|---|
| 8. | network | | h. a device that sends data and information over a computer |
| 9. | Internet Service Provider (ISP) | | i. a very large computer that connects other computers with each other |
| 10. | HTTP/HTML | | j. part of a computer that locate web pages for users |

*Congratulations! You have completed this lesson.*

Answer the question in complete sentences.

1. What is the difference between the Internet and the WWW?

   _____

   _____

   _____

   _____

2. What is the difference between a modem and a router?

   _____

   _____

   _____

   _____

**Lesson 6**

# Lesson 6: Housing Vocabulary

Look at the illustration. What do you think the vocabulary words mean? Predict a meaning based on the illustration.

| # | Vocabulary Words | Predicted Meaning | Illustration |
|---|---|---|---|
| 1. | utilities not included | _____ _____ _____ | |
| 2. | offer to purchase | _____ _____ _____ | |
| 3. | walkout bungalow | _____ _____ _____ | |
| 4. | one-year lease | _____ _____ _____ | |
| 5. | property manager | _____ _____ _____ | |

# Lesson 6 — Housing Vocabulary

Name: _____

| # | Vocabulary Words | Predicted Meaning | Illustration |
|---|---|---|---|
| 6. | attached garage | | |
| 7. | rental agreement | | |
| 8. | one bedroom and den | | |
| 9. | possession date | | |
| 10. | unfurnished suite | | |

**Lesson 6** Housing Vocabulary  Name:

## Fill in the Blanks:

Use the vocabulary words to fill in the blanks with the correct answers. Use each answer once.

| utilities not included | offer to purchase | walkout bungalow | one year lease | property manager |
| attached garage | rental agreement | one bedroom and den | possession date | unfurnished suite |

1. I have my own furniture, so I will be renting an _____.

2. On the _____, we will be moving into our new home.

3. There is a _____ for rent on the next floor.

4. Keep your _____ in a safe place in case you need it.

5. It is better to have an _____ than a detached one.

6. Call the _____ if the heat doesn't come on soon.

7. I will only sign a _____ as next year I want to buy my own house.

8. I prefer a _____ to a two-story home.

9. When you decide which house you want to buy, make an _____ to the owner.

10. There may be some extra charges because the ad says _____ _____.

**Lesson 6** — Housing Vocabulary          Name:

# Find the Meaning:

Match the Vocabulary Words with the meanings. Write the correct letter in the answer column.

| # | Vocabulary Words | Answer | Meanings |
|---|---|---|---|
| 1. | utilities not included | | a. Tenants must pay their own electricity, heating, water, etc. |
| 2. | offer to purchase | | b. The renter signs an agreement to rent the property for a period of one year. |
| 3. | walkout bungalow | | c. The garage is attached to the house. |
| 4. | one-year lease | | d. the date on which a purchaser becomes the owner of a property |
| 5. | property manager | | e. The suite is rented without furniture. |
| 6. | attached garage | | f. There is one bedroom and one den. |
| 7. | rental agreement | | g. The purchaser offers to buy the property for a specified price and under certain conditions. |

**Lesson 6** — Housing Vocabulary — Name:

| # | Vocabulary Words | Answer | Meanings |
|---|---|---|---|
| 8. | one bedroom and den | _____ | h. the person who manages the business or other issues related to a property |
| 9. | possession date | _____ | i. a house on one floor with an elevated basement that contains an outdoor entrance |
| 10. | unfurnished suite | _____ | j. a written document that states the conditions under which a person rents a property |

*Congratulations! You have completed this lesson.*

Write a conversation between a person applying to rent an apartment and a property manager. Use the vocabulary words in your conversation.

_____
_____
_____
_____
_____
_____
_____

# Lesson 7: Laundry and Dry-Cleaning Vocabulary

Look at the illustration. What do you think the vocabulary words mean? Predict a meaning based on the illustration.

| # | Vocabulary Words | Predicted Meaning | Illustration |
|---|---|---|---|
| 1. | stain didn't come out | | |
| 2. | front-loading washing machine | | |
| 3. | top-loading washing machine | | |
| 4. | lint container | | |
| 5. | Wash in cold water. | | |

| Lesson 7 | Laundry and Dry-Cleaning Vocabulary | Name: |

| # | Vocabulary Words | Predicted Meaning | Illustration |
|---|---|---|---|
| 6. | white clothes only | _____ _____ _____ | |
| 7. | Do not bleach. | _____ _____ _____ | |
| 8. | Hang to dry. | _____ _____ _____ | |
| 9. | fabric softener | _____ _____ _____ | |
| 10. | extra rinse | _____ _____ _____ | |

42  OTM18113  ISBN: 9781770788725 © On The Mark Press

**Lesson 7** — Laundry and Dry-Cleaning Vocabulary        Name:

## Fill in the Blanks:

Use the vocabulary words to fill in the blanks with the correct answers. Use each answer once.

| stain didn't come out | front-loading washing machine | top-loading washing machine | lint container | Wash in cold water. |
|---|---|---|---|---|
| white clothes only | Do not bleach. | Hang to dry. | fabric softener | extra rinse |

1. The dry cleaners tried very hard but the _____.

2. Please don't put any dark clothes in this basket because it is for _____.

3. In the _____, you can watch the clothes as they go through the cycles.

4. I don't want these jeans ruined, so _____.

5. Put the cover down on the _____; please, I am ready to wash the clothes.

6. Those sweaters don't go in the dryer, just _____.

7. The _____ was full when I emptied it yesterday.

8. I always use _____ for the baby's diapers and other clothes.

9. The tag says to _____ to avoid shrinkage.

10. Put this load through an _____ if that fabric makes you itch.

**Lesson 7** Laundry and Dry-Cleaning Vocabulary     Name:

## Find the Meaning:

Match the Vocabulary Words with the meanings. Write the correct letter in the answer column.

| # | Vocabulary Words | Answer | Meanings |
|---|---|---|---|
| 1. | stain didn't come out | | a. The stain or mark in the material is still there. |
| 2. | front-loading washing machine | | b. a small compartment where the lint collects in the dryer |
| 3. | top-loading washing machine | | c. Wash white clothes only in this cycle. |
| 4. | lint container | | d. Hang the clothes up to dry. |
| 5. | Wash in cold water. | | e. Do not add bleach when washing the clothes. |
| 6. | white clothes only | | f. Load the clothes at the front of the machine. |
| 7. | Do not bleach. | | g. Load the clothes at the top of the machine. |

**Lesson 7**  Laundry and Dry-Cleaning Vocabulary   Name:

| # | Vocabulary Words | Answer | Meanings |
|---|---|---|---|
| 8. | Hang to dry. | _____ | h. Wash the material in cold water. |
| 9. | fabric softener | _____ | i. liquid added to the wash cycle or paper-like material added to the dryer used to make the clothes come out softer |
| 10. | extra rinse | _____ | j. Use the rinse cycle an extra time. |

*Congratulations! You have completed this lesson.*

Circle the correct answer.

1. White clothes only means:
   a. Only add white clothes to the laundry.
   b. Add white clothes to the other clothes in the laundry.
   c. Do not add white clothes to the laundry.

# Lesson 8: Education and Career Vocabulary

Look at the illustration. What do you think the vocabulary words mean? Predict a meaning based on the illustration.

| # | Vocabulary Words | Predicted Meaning | Illustration |
|---|---|---|---|
| 1. | ESL course | _____ | |
| 2. | deadline | _____ | |
| 3. | participation mark | _____ | |
| 4. | answer booklet | _____ | |
| 5. | post-secondary education | _____ | |

| Lesson 8 | Education and Career Vocabulary | Name: |
|---|---|---|

| # | Vocabulary Words | Predicted Meaning | Illustration |
|---|---|---|---|
| 6. | semester | | |
| 7. | fall term | | |
| 8. | revise your paper | | |
| 9. | multiple choice exam | | |
| 10. | Hand in your test. | | |

**Lesson 8** — Education and Career Vocabulary          Name:

## Fill in the Blanks:

Use the vocabulary words to fill in the blanks with the correct answers. Use each answer once.

| ESL course | deadline | participation mark | answer booklet | post- secondary education |
| semester | fall term | Revise your paper. | multiple choice exam | Hand in your test. |

1. Please _____ before handing it to the instructor.

2. In order to get a good _____, it is important to answer questions in class.

3. In September, I registered for the _____.

4. The _____ for handing in the essay is tomorrow.

5. I would rather take a _____ than a short answer test.

6. Put your names on the _____.

7. You can _____ when you are finished.

8. When I finish high school, I will begin my _____ at the community college.

9. Last _____, I took math and biology.

10. To learn English reading and writing, sign up for the _____.

**Lesson 8** — Education and Career Vocabulary  Name:

## Find the Meaning:

Match the Vocabulary Words with the meanings. Write the correct letter in the answer column.

| # | Vocabulary Words | Answer | Meanings |
|---|---|---|---|
| 1. | ESL course | | a. the booklet used for placing answers to a quiz or test |
| 2. | Deadline | | b. a mark given for taking part or contributing in class |
| 3. | participation mark | | c. the date at which the assignment must be handed in to the instructor |
| 4. | answer booklet | | d. English as a Second Language course taken to learn the English language |
| 5. | post-secondary | | e. a test in which students choose one correct answer on a test or exam |
| 6. | Semester | | f. Make changes to improve the paper. |
| 7. | fall term | | g. courses taken in the fall of the year |

**Lesson 8**  Education and Career Vocabulary   Name:

| # | Vocabulary Words | Answer | Meanings |
|---|---|---|---|
| 8. | Revise your paper. | _____ | h. a period of time during which a course is offered |
| 9. | multiple choice exam | _____ | i. education taken after completing high-school |
| 10. | Hand in your test. | _____ | j. Give the test to the instructor. |

*Congratulations! You have completed this lesson.*

Write an email to a classmate, offering advice for writing a test. Use the vocabulary words in your email.

_____

_____

_____

_____

_____

_____

# Lesson 9: Law Vocabulary

Look at the illustration. What do you think the vocabulary words mean? Predict a meaning based on the illustration.

| # | Vocabulary Words | Predicted Meaning | Illustration |
|---|---|---|---|
| 1. | under arrest | | |
| 2. | suspect | | |
| 3. | under investigation | | |
| 4. | speeding ticket | | |
| 5. | parking ticket | | |

| Lesson 9 | Law Vocabulary | Name: |
| --- | --- | --- |

| # | Vocabulary Words | Predicted Meaning | Illustration |
| --- | --- | --- | --- |
| 6. | court date | | |
| 7. | hire a lawyer | | |
| 8. | burglary | | |
| 9. | identity theft | | |
| 10. | vandalism | | |

**Lesson 9** — Law Vocabulary        Name:

## Fill in the Blanks:

Use the vocabulary words to fill in the blanks with the correct answers. Use each answer once.

| under arrest | suspect | under investigation | speeding ticket | parking ticket |
|---|---|---|---|---|
| court date | hire a lawyer | burglary | identity theft | vandalism |

1. When the impaired driver got out of the car, the police told him he was _____.

2. There have been many instances of _____ in the neighbourhood this weekend.

3. This is the third _____ I have received on this street.

4. When is your _____? I want to come and support you.

5. Last night, there was a _____ at the electronics store.

6. The kidnapping has been _____ since last month.

7. You will get a _____ if you don't slow down.

8. Is that man the police are talking to a _____?

9. She got a letter from the bank concerning an issue of _____.

10. I would advise you to _____ to help you with this case.

**Lesson 9** — Law Vocabulary          Name:

## Find the Meaning:

Match the Vocabulary Words with the meanings. Write the correct letter in the answer column.

| # | Vocabulary Words | Answer | Meanings |
|---|---|---|---|
| 1. | under arrest | _____ | a. a piece of paper saying the person must pay an amount of money called a fine for exceeding the speeding limit |
| 2. | suspect | _____ | b. a situation that the police are trying to solve |
| 3. | under investigation | _____ | c. a person the police think may have committed a crime |
| 4. | speeding ticket | _____ | d. The police have taken the person into custody. |
| 5. | parking ticket | _____ | e. using the identity of another person in order to make money or gain in another way |
| 6. | court date | _____ | f. entering the property of another person in order to steal items |
| 7. | hire a lawyer | _____ | g. to pay for the services of a lawyer |

**Lesson 9**  Law Vocabulary   Name:

| # | Vocabulary Words | Answer | Meanings |
|---|---|---|---|
| 8. | burglary | _____ | h. the date at which a person must appear in court |
| 9. | identity theft | _____ | i. a piece of paper saying the person must pay an amount of money for parking in a no parking location |
| 10. | vandalism | _____ | j. acts that damage property |

*Congratulations! You have completed this lesson.*

Use these vocabulary words in sentences.

1. identity theft
2. suspect
3. vandalism
4. court date
5. burglary

Lesson 10

# Lesson 10: Government Vocabulary

Look at the illustration. What do you think the vocabulary words mean? Predict a meaning based on the illustration.

| # | Vocabulary Words | Predicted Meaning | Illustration |
|---|---|---|---|
| 1. | parliament | | |
| 2. | bill | | |
| 3. | constituency | | |
| 4. | senator | | |
| 5. | riding | | |

| # | Vocabulary Words | Predicted Meaning | Illustration |
|---|---|---|---|
| 6. | election | | |
| 7. | premier | | |
| 8. | cabinet minister | | |
| 9. | law | | |
| 10. | mayor | | |

Lesson 10  Government Vocabulary  Name:

**Lesson 10**  Government Vocabulary       Name:

## Fill in the Blanks:

Use the vocabulary words to fill in the blanks with the correct answers. Use each answer once.

| parliament | bill | constituency | senator | riding |
| election | premier | cabinet minister | law | mayor |

1. After he served for many years in parliament, he went on to become a _____.

2. The bill became _____ this morning.

3. The officials haven't passed the _____ yet.

4. The _____ selected his cabinet after the election.

5. I don't live in that _____, but I know the candidates for the election.

6. The _____ in charge of education will visit the schools today.

7. Who is the _____ of this town?

8. The _____ will be held on October 15th this year.

9. A _____ is the same as a constituency.

10. Did you know she became a member of _____ last week?

**Lesson 10** Government Vocabulary      Name:

## Find the Meaning:

Match the Vocabulary Words with the meanings. Write the correct letter in the answer column.

| # | Vocabulary Words | Answer | Meanings |
|---|---|---|---|
| 1. | parliament | | a. Canadian government body that makes the laws |
| 2. | bill | | b. a recommendation for a law that needs to be passed before becoming a law |
| 3. | constituency | | c. rules that citizens must follow |
| 4. | senator | | d. the head of a town or city government |
| 5. | riding | | e. the head of one of the government departments in Canada |
| 6. | election | | f. the leader of a provincial government |
| 7. | premier | | g. the area represented by a member of parliament in Canada |

**Lesson 10** Government Vocabulary  Name:

| # | Vocabulary Words | Answer | Meanings |
|---|---|---|---|
| 8. | cabinet minister | _____ | h. appointed members of the Senate in Canada |
| 9. | law | _____ | i. another name for a constituency |
| 10. | mayor | _____ | j. a procedure in which citizens vote for leaders of the country |

*Congratulations! You have completed this lesson.*

Write a news article about the upcoming election. Use the vocabulary words in your writing.

_____
_____
_____
_____
_____
_____
_____
_____

# Lesson 11: Job and Interview Vocabulary

Look at the illustration. What do you think the vocabulary words mean? Predict a meaning based on the illustration.

| # | Vocabulary Words | Predicted Meaning | Illustration |
|---|---|---|---|
| 1. | Webcam job interview | | |
| 2. | entry-level position | | |
| 3. | job interview | | |
| 4. | cover letter | | |
| 5. | senior level position | | |

**Lesson 11**  Job and Interview Vocabulary     Name:

| # | Vocabulary Words | Predicted Meaning | Illustration |
|---|---|---|---|
| 6. | thank-you letter | | |
| 7. | Arrive on time. | | |
| 8. | career goals | | |
| 9. | Take notes. | | |
| 10. | Practise for the interview. | | |

**Lesson 11**  Job and Interview Vocabulary        Name:

## Fill in the Blanks:

Use the vocabulary words to fill in the blanks with the correct answers. Use each answer once.

| Webcam job interview | entry-level position | job interview | cover letter | senior level position |
|---|---|---|---|---|
| thank you letter | Arrive on time. | career goals | Take notes. | Practise for the interview. |

1. You will need to submit a _____ with that resume.

2. I have a lot of experience, so I should qualify for a _____ in this company.

3. There will be a lot of information shared at the meeting, so don't forget to _____.

4. My brother told me to _____ in order to overcome the nervousness.

5. The company wants a _____ rather than interviewing me face to face.

6. Would you help me write a _____ for the interview?

7. When you finish your course, apply for an _____ at this company.

8. I have to go because I want to _____ for the interview.

9. Have you considered your _____ in seeking this position?

10. Do you have a _____ with this organization?

**Lesson 11** Job and Interview Vocabulary  Name:

## Find the Meaning:

Match the Vocabulary Words with the meanings. Write the correct letter in the answer column.

| # | Vocabulary Words | Answer | Meanings |
|---|---|---|---|
| 1. | Webcam job interview | | a. interview held over the internet that uses a Webcam camera |
| 2. | entry-level position | | b. a position for inexperienced employees entering the workforce at a particular job |
| 3. | job interview | | c. a meeting undertaken to answer questions related to job suitability |
| 4. | cover letter | | d. practise discussing job skills and requirements before the interview |
| 5. | senior level position | | e. writing down important points or questions mentioned in the interview |
| 6. | thank-you letter | | f. career plans a job applicant has for the future |
| 7. | Arrive on time. | | g. letter sent to an organization or business thanking them for an interview |

**Lesson 11** Job and Interview Vocabulary    Name:

| # | Vocabulary Words | Answer | Meanings |
|---|---|---|---|
| 8. | career goals | _____ | h. h. to arrive at the time the interview begins. |
| 9. | Take notes. | _____ | i. i. job position requiring leadership ability and skills |
| 10. | Practise for the interview. | _____ | j. j. a letter of introduction sent to a potential employer |

*Congratulations! You have completed this lesson.*

Write a thank-you letter to a business that interviewed you for a position. Use the vocabulary words in your letter.

_____
_____
_____
_____
_____
_____
_____
_____

**Lesson 12**

# Lesson 12: Social Networking Vocabulary

Look at the illustration. What do you think the vocabulary words mean? Predict a meaning based on the illustration.

| # | Vocabulary Words | Predicted Meaning | Illustration |
|---|---|---|---|
| 1. | social networking | | |
| 2. | friends | | |
| 3. | followers | | |
| 4. | connections | | |
| 5. | Facebook | | |

| Lesson 12 | Social Networking Vocabulary | Name: |

| # | Vocabulary Words | Predicted Meaning | Illustration |
|---|---|---|---|
| 6. | FaceTime | | |
| 7. | Instagram | | |
| 8. | social media networks | | |
| 9. | Tweet | | |
| 10. | Circles | | |

**Lesson 12**  Social Networking Vocabulary  Name:

## Fill in the Blanks:

Use the vocabulary words to fill in the blanks with the correct answers. Use each answer once.

| social networking | friends | followers | connections | Facebook |
| FaceTime | Instagram | social media network | Tweet | circles |

1. My oldest sister made a _____ on Twitter before she went to school.

2. Are those girls part of the _____ on Google?

3. Which category do those _____ belong to on LinkedIn?

4. I have been using _____ to communicate with my friends and family for several years.

5. Facebook reminds me of my _____ who have made requests on a regular basis.

6. Those photos of my holidays were made and shared on _____.

7. I rely upon my _____ for friendship and communication.

8. Since the beginning of this year, I have added a lot of _____ to my social media network.

9. Do you get most of your _____ calls on your phone or iPad?

10. Since I started _____, it has been easier for me to keep in touch with my old classmates.

**Lesson 12** — Social Networking Vocabulary        Name:

## Find the Meaning:

Match the Vocabulary Words with the meanings. Write the correct letter in the answer column.

| # | Vocabulary Words | Answer | Meanings |
|---|---|---|---|
| 1. | social networking | | a. an application for taking and sharing photos |
| 2. | friends | | b. social relationships with others that take place over the internet |
| 3. | followers | | c. posts made on Twitter, a social media website |
| 4. | connections | | d. groups of friends, family and others on a social network called Google |
| 5. | Facebook | | e. an online platform in which people interact socially with other people |
| 6. | FaceTime | | f. a term used on Facebook for the people followed on that platform |
| 7. | Instagram | | g. persons who enroll in the account of another person |

**Lesson 12**  Social Networking Vocabulary    Name:

| # | Vocabulary Words | Answer | Meanings |
|---|---|---|---|
| 8. | social media network | _____ | h. contacts on LinkedIn that appear in three different categories |
| 9. | Tweet | _____ | i. a social media platform connecting people with others |
| 10. | Circles | _____ | j. an application for making and receiving video and audio calls using Apple technology |

*Congratulations! You have completed this lesson.*

Make a Personal Dictionary for these words. Use your own words.

1. Social media network
2. Friends
3. Connections
4. Instagram
5. Circles

# Lesson 13: Fitness and Health Vocabulary

Look at the illustration. What do you think the vocabulary words mean? Predict a meaning based on the illustration.

| # | Vocabulary Words | Predicted Meaning | Illustration |
|---|---|---|---|
| 1. | recreational centre | | |
| 2. | fitness membership | | |
| 3. | membership expired | | |
| 4. | membership renewal | | |
| 5. | personal trainer | | |

| # | Vocabulary Words | Predicted Meaning | Illustration |
|---|---|---|---|
| 6. | fitness instructor | | |
| 7. | change room | | |
| 8. | aerobics class | | |
| 9. | drop-in rate | | |
| 10. | elliptical machine | | |

**Lesson 13** Fitness and Health Vocabulary    Name:

## Fill in the Blanks:

Use the vocabulary words to fill in the blanks with the correct answers. Use each answer once.

| recreational centre | fitness membership | membership expired | membership renewal | personal trainer |
|---|---|---|---|---|
| fitness instructor | change room | aerobics class | drop-in rate | elliptical machine |

1. The _____ says I should sign up for her aerobics class.

2. Meet me at the _____ in front of the swimming pool.

3. I tripped and fell today while taking my _____.

4. I can't go to the recreational centre today because my _____.

5. Are you going to buy a regular or enhanced _____ _____?

6. The recreation centre sent me a notice to complete a _____ _____ before the end of the month.

7. Did you leave your bathing suit in the _____?

8. In the long run, if you pay the _____, it costs more than obtaining a membership.

9. First I use the _____, then I go on the treadmill.

10. The _____ showed me how to lift the weights properly.

**Lesson 13** — Fitness and Health Vocabulary          Name:

# Find the Meaning:

Match the Vocabulary Words with the meanings. Write the correct letter in the answer column.

| # | Vocabulary Words | Answer | Meanings |
|---|---|---|---|
| 1. | recreational centre | | a. a machine which allows users to make movements of step climbing, walking or jogging |
| 2. | fitness membership | | b. fee charged when a person without a membership attends a recreational centre |
| 3. | membership expired | | c. the membership is no longer valid |
| 4. | membership renewal | | d. making the membership active again |
| 5. | personal trainer | | e. a building where people go to engage in sports and other leisure activities |
| 6. | fitness instructor | | f. a person who instructs others in fitness classes |
| 7. | change room | | g. a room set aside at a recreational centre for changing clothing |

# Lesson 13 — Fitness and Health Vocabulary

Name: _____

| # | Vocabulary Words | Answer | Meanings |
|---|---|---|---|
| 8. | aerobics class | _____ | h. a class aimed at improving the circulatory system |
| 9. | drop-in rate | _____ | i. belonging to a fitness centre by paying a certain fee |
| 10. | elliptical machine | _____ | j. a certified person hired to assist with fitness activities |

*Congratulations! You have completed this lesson.*

Make up an ad that advertises the services offered at a recreation centre that has just opened in your community.

_____

_____

_____

_____

_____

_____

_____

_____

Lesson 14

# Lesson 14: Hobbies and Entertainment Vocabulary

Look at the illustration. What do you think the vocabulary words mean? Predict a meaning based on the illustration.

| # | Vocabulary Words | Predicted Meaning | Illustration |
|---|---|---|---|
| 1. | symphony | | |
| 2. | art gallery | | |
| 3. | dinner theatre | | |
| 4. | exhibition | | |
| 5. | jazz concert | | |

**Lesson 14**    Hobbies and Entertainment Vocabulary    Name:

| # | Vocabulary Words | Predicted Meaning | Illustration |
|---|---|---|---|
| 6. | movie theatre | | |
| 7. | museum | | |
| 8. | opera | | |
| 9. | children's game centre | | |
| 10. | children's indoor playground | | |

**Lesson 14** Hobbies and Entertainment Vocabulary    Name:

## Fill in the Blanks:

Use the vocabulary words to fill in the blanks with the correct answers. Use each answer once.

| symphony | art gallery | dinner theatre | exhibition | jazz concert |
| movie theatre | museum | opera | children's game centre | children's indoor playground |

1. On holidays, I like to take my children to the _____ _____ to exercise.

2. Every weekend, my son asks to go to the _____ _____ to play his favourite video games.

3. Our cousin is a renowned _____ singer.

4. At the history _____, I saw a replica of one of the first airplanes.

5. Did you bring enough money to buy popcorn at the _____.

6. My grandma loves classical piano music, so she will enjoy the _____ this weekend.

7. At the _____, I noticed some sculptures I hadn't seen before.

8. The first time I saw that play was at the _____.

9. There is a home show and _____ this weekend at the arena.

10. Grandpa will be playing his saxophone at the _____ tonight.

**Lesson 14** Hobbies and Entertainment Vocabulary  Name:

## Find the Meaning:

Match the Vocabulary Words with the meanings. Write the correct letter in the answer column.

| # | Vocabulary Words | Answer | Meanings |
|---|---|---|---|
| 1. | symphony | | a. attending a concert featuring jazz music |
| 2. | art gallery | | b. eating dinner and watching a play |
| 3. | dinner theatre | | c. attending a classical music concert |
| 4. | exhibition | | d. a building where historic items are displayed |
| 5. | jazz concert | | e. a building where children play a variety of types of games |
| 6. | movie theatre | | f. a place where items are displayed |
| 7. | museum | | g. building that displays paintings and other forms of art |

**Lesson 14**  Hobbies and Entertainment Vocabulary    Name:

| # | Vocabulary Words | Answer | Meanings |
|---|---|---|---|
| 8. | Opera | _____ | h. also called the cinema, a place to watch movies |
| 9. | children's game centre | _____ | i. form of entertainment in which performers sing and act |
| 10. | children's indoor playground | _____ | j. a place where children enjoy indoor playground activities |

*Congratulations! You have completed this lesson.*

Write or create a travel article about entertainment available in your town or city.

_____
_____
_____
_____
_____
_____
_____
_____

# Lesson 15: Food Safety Vocabulary

Look at the illustration. What do you think the vocabulary words mean? Predict a meaning based on the illustration.

| # | Vocabulary Words | Predicted Meaning | Illustration |
|---|---|---|---|
| 1. | right temperature | | |
| 2. | Keep refrigerated. | | |
| 3. | Use separate utensils. | | |
| 4. | Refrigerate after opening. | | |
| 5. | best before date | | |

**Lesson 15** Food Safety Vocabulary  Name: _____

| # | Vocabulary Words | Predicted Meaning | Illustration |
|---|---|---|---|
| 6. | Wash your hands thoroughly. | | |
| 7. | expiration date | | |
| 8. | bacteria | | |
| 9. | contaminants | | |
| 10. | allergens | | |

**Lesson 15** Food Safety Vocabulary     Name: _____

## Fill in the Blanks:

Use the vocabulary words to fill in the blanks with the correct answers. Use each answer once.

| right temperature | Keep refrigerated. | Use separate utensils. | Refrigerate after opening. | best before date |
|---|---|---|---|---|
| Wash your hands thoroughly. | expiration date | bacteria | contaminants | allergens |

1. Use a thermometer to see if the meat is at the _____ _____.

2. Harmful _____ formed in the meat that was left out on the counter.

3. Be sure to read the _____ on the salad dressing.

4. The _____ in tomatoes make my face swell.

5. It is important to _____ before handling food.

6. The _____ in the leftover dressing probably made you sick.

7. What is the _____ on the milk?

8. When making those meals, be sure to _____ when stirring the food.

9. On the carton of cream, it says to _____.

10. _____ that bottle of mayonnaise.

**Lesson 15** Food Safety Vocabulary   Name:

## Find the Meaning:

Match the Vocabulary Words with the meanings. Write the correct letter in the answer column.

| # | Vocabulary Words | Answer | Meanings |
|---|---|---|---|
| 1. | right temperature | | a. the temperature needed to cook the food item |
| 2. | Keep refrigerated. | | b. using different utensils for each cooking task |
| 3. | Use separate utensils. | | c. the date at which items are freshest and safest |
| 4. | Refrigerate after opening. | | d. the date at which an item can no longer be used |
| 5. | best before date | | e. unwanted substances that cause harm |
| 6. | Wash your hands thoroughly. | | f. substances that cause uncomfortable reactions in particular individuals |
| 7. | expiration date | | g. keeping items in the refrigerator |

**Lesson 15** Food Safety Vocabulary            Name:

| # | Vocabulary Words | Answer | Meanings |
|---|---|---|---|
| 8. | bacteria | _____ | h. after opening, keeping these items in the refrigerator |
| 9. | contaminants | _____ | i. washing the hands carefully |
| 10. | allergens | _____ | j. microorganisms that can cause diseases |

*Congratulations! You have completed this lesson.*

Make up a personal dictionary for these words.

1. Allergens
2. Contaminants
3. Bacteria
4. Best before date
5. Use separate utensils

# Answer Key

**LESSON 1: Page 11**

**Fill in the Blanks: Page 13**

1. high water level 2. dogs on leash 3. speed bumps 4. do not pass 5. detour
6. school crossing 7. watch for wildlife 8. handicapped parking 9. merge
10. hill warning

**Find the Meaning: Page 14**

1. E  2. G  3. A  4. F  5. B  6. H  7. C  8. I  9. D  10. J

Words with prefixes or suffixes--dangerous, handicapped, crossing, leashes, parking, detour

**LESSON 2: Page 16**

**Fill in the Blanks: Page 18**

1. Daylight Time 2. Eastern Time 3. time zones 4. Mountain Time
5. Newfoundland Time 6. Pacific Time 7. Standard Time 8. Central Time
9. Yukon Time 10. Atlantic Time

**Find the Meaning: Page 19**

1. G  2. F  3. C  4. B  5. A  6. D  7. E  8. I  9. H  10. J

**Multiple Choice: Page 20**

1-C  2-C

**LESSON 3: Page 21**

**Fill in the Blanks: Page 23**

1. jumper cables 2. defroster 3. model 4. vehicle registration 5. sedan
6. snow tires 7. SUV 8. liability insurance 9. collision insurance 10. oil check

**Find the Meaning: Page 24**

1. B  2. C  3. G  4. H  5. I  6. E  7. F  8. J  9. D  10. A

**LESSON 4: Page 26**

**Fill in the Blanks: Page 28**

1. store at room temperature 2. refills 0 3. syringe 4. one capsule three times a day 5. dropper 6. avoid direct sunlight 7. expires January, 2018 8. may cause drowsiness 9. over the counter 10. generic

**Find the Meaning: Page 29**

1. A  2. E  3. F  4. I  5. B  6. J  7. G  8. H  9. D  10. C

Misspelled words: syringe, medication, drowsiness, dropper

**LESSON 5: Page 31**

**Fill in the Blanks: Page 33**

1. network 2. server 3. router 4. Internet Service Provider (ISP) 5. search engine
6. WWW 7. Internet 8. HTTP/HTML 9. modem 10. Web browser

**Find the Meaning: Page 34**
  1. A   2. G   3. I   4. B   5. H   6. C   7. J   8. F   9. D   10. E

## LESSON 6: Page 36
**Fill in the Blanks: Page 38**
  1. unfurnished suite 2. possession date 3. one bedroom and den
  4. rental agreement 5. attached garage 6. property manager 7. one year lease
  8. walkout bungalow 9. offer to purchase 10. utilities not included

**Find the Meaning: Page 39**
  1. A   2. G   3. I   4. B   5. H   6. C   7. J   8. F   9. D   10. E

## LESSON 7: Page 41
**Fill in the Blanks: Page 43**
  1. stain didn't come out 2. white clothes only 3. front-loading washing machine
  4. do not bleach 5. top-loading washing machine 6. hang to dry
  7. lint container 8. fabric softener 9. wash in cold water 10. extra rinse

**Find the Meaning: Page 44**
  1. A   2. F   3. G   4. B   5. H   6. C   7. E   8. D   9. I   10. J

**Multiple Choice: Page 45**
  1-A

## LESSON 8: Page 46
**Fill in the Blanks: Page 48**
  1. revise your paper 2. participation mark 3. fall term 4. deadline
  5. multiple choice exam 6. answer booklet 7. hand in your test
  8. post-secondary education 9. semester 10. ESL course

**Find the Meaning: Page 49**
  1. D   2. C   3. B   4. A   5. I   6. H   7. G   8. F   9. E   10. J

## LESSON 9: Page 51
**Fill in the Blanks: Page 53**
  1. under arrest 2. vandalism 3. parking ticket 4. court date 5. burglary
  6. under investigation 7. speeding ticket 8. suspect 9. identity theft
  10. hire a lawyer

**Find the Meaning: Page 54**
  1. D   2. C   3. B   4. A   5. I   6. H   7. G   8. F   9. E   10. J

## LESSON 10: Page 56
**Fill in the Blanks: Page 58**
  1. senator 2. law 3. bill 4. premier 5. constituency 6. cabinet minister
  7. mayor 8. election 9. riding 10. parliament

# Answer Key

**Find the Meaning: Page 59**
1. A  2. B  3. G  4. H  5. I  6. J  7. F  8. E  9. C  10. D

## LESSON 11: Page 61

**Fill in the Blanks: Page 63**
1. cover letter 2. senior level position 3. take notes 4. practice for the interview 5. Webcam job interview 6. thank you letter 7. entry-level position 8. arrive on time 9. career goals 10. job interview

**Find the Meaning: Page 64**
1. A  2. B  3. C  4. J  5. I  6. G  7. H  8. F  9. E  10. D

## LESSON 12: Page 66

**Fill in the Blanks: Page 68**
1. Tweet 2. circles 3. connections 4. Facebook 5. friends 6. Instagram 7. social media network 8. followers 9. Facetime 10. social networking

**Find the Meaning: Page 69**
1. E  2. F  3. G  4. H  5. I  6. J  7. A  8. B  9. C  10. D

## LESSON 13: Page 71

**Fill in the Blanks: Page 73**
1. fitness instructor 2. recreational centre 3. aerobics class 4. membership expired 5. fitness membership 6. membership renewal 7. change room 8. drop-in rate 9. elliptical machine 10. personal trainer

**Find the Meaning: Page 74**
1. E  2. I  3. C  4. D  5. J  6. F  7. G  8. H  9. B  10. A

## LESSON 14: Page 76

**Fill in the Blanks: Page 78**
1. children's indoor playground 2. children's game centre 3. opera 4. museum 5. movie theatre 6. symphony 7. art gallery 8. dinner theatre 9. exhibition 10. jazz concert

**Find the Meaning: Page 79**
1. C  2. G  3. B  4. F  5. A  6. H  7. D  8. I  9. E  10. J

## LESSON 15: Page 81

**Fill in the Blanks: Page 83**
1. right temperature 2. bacteria 3. best before date 4. allergens 5. wash your hands thoroughly 6. contaminants 7. expiration date 8. separate utensils 9. keep refrigerated 10. refrigerate after opening

**Find the Meaning: Page 84**
1. A  2. G  3. B  4. H  5. C  6. I  7. D  8. J  9. E  10. F

www.ingramcontent.com/pod-product-compliance
Lightning Source LLC
Chambersburg PA
CBHW080438230426
43662CB00015B/2312